I BELIEVE!

Apostles' Creed Wordplays

ANITA REITH STOHS

ILLUSTRATED BY
GORDON WILLMAN

CPH
SAINT LOUIS

To Louis John, who puts Acts 10:34–36 into action

Scripture quotations taken from the HOLY BIBLE, NEW INTERNATIONAL VERSION®. NIV®. Copyright © 1973, 1978, 1984 by International Bible Society. Used by permission of Zondervan Publishing House. All rights reserved.

Text copyright © 2000 Anita Reith Stohs
Illustrations copyright © 2000 Concordia Publishing House

Published by Concordia Publishing House
3558 S. Jefferson Avenue, St. Louis, MO 63118-3968
Manufactured in the United States of America

2   3   4   5   6   7   8   9   10   o9   08   07   06   05   04   03   02   01

Contents

I BELIEVE

THE APOSTLES' CREED

For almost 2,000 years, Christians have used these words to tell what they believe about God and why they trust in Him. We call these words the "Apostles' Creed." A creed is a statement of faith.

I believe in God, **the Father** Almighty, maker of heaven and earth. And in **Jesus Christ**, His only Son, our Lord, who was conceived by the Holy Spirit, born of the virgin Mary, suffered under Pontius Pilate, was crucified, died, and was buried. He descended into hell. The third day He rose again from the dead. He ascended into heaven and sits at the right hand of God the Father Almighty. From thence He will come to judge the living and the dead.

I believe in **the Holy Spirit**, the holy Christian Church, the communion of saints, the forgiveness of sins, the resurrection of the body, and the life everlasting. Amen.

THE GOD I KNOW AND TRUST

The wordplays in this book will help you learn what the Bible teaches about the God you know and trust.

Find and circle these words from the Apostles' Creed. Be sure to look up-and-down and back-and-forth.

WORD BANK

ALMIGHTY
BODY
BURIED
CHRIST
CHURCH
CRUCIFIED
DEAD
DESCENDED
EARTH
EVERLASTING
FATHER
GOD
HEAVEN
HOLY
JESUS
JUDGE
LIFE
LORD
MAKER
MARY
PILATE
RIGHT
ROSE
SAINTS
SON
SPIRIT
SUFFERED

```
A S C D E T E E T A L I P U P I H C R U H C
I A G O D B E L I B U R I E D E I U M A K H
D I E V E R L A S T I N G F X J E G D U J U
E N H H G T S I R H C O R A T O R U H D O B
R T E E W A R I P S Y L E T H R O S E X E O
E S F A T L I R E K A M H H E R Y L O H C D
F R E V H M G H S O U R I E R O S C N E O Y
F A D E A D L T U G S E D R M C I O U A M S
U A N R E H I Y S E O A L M I G H T Y V T P
S N E V A F F M E D N T D E S C E N D E D I
E D H T R A E A J R D R O L M X O S W N Q X
A M A R Y O R K E Q O L T G R I G H T M G T
R T H R D E I F I C U R C I F D S P I R I T
```

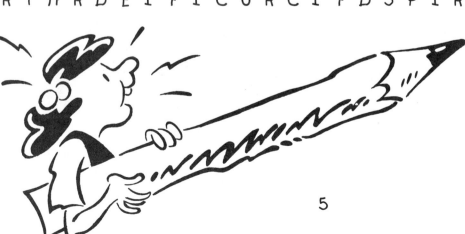

5

A WONDERFUL GOD

What a wonderful God we have. The Bible uses many words to describe God. Some of these words are listed below. Place these words about God into the crossword puzzle below. God is all these and more!

WORD BANK

ALMIGHTY
ETERNAL
FAIR
FAITHFUL
FORGIVING
GOOD

UNCHANGEABLE
HOLY
JUST
KIND
LOVE
MERCIFUL
SPIRIT

6

GOD IS THREE PERSONS

God is three Persons—Father, Son, and Holy Spirit—in one God. We call this God the "Holy Trinity" or "Triune God." This means "Three-in-One." You may have noticed that baptisms are done in the name of the Father, the Son, and the Holy Spirit.

Find and circle these words in the word search below. Be sure to look up-and-down and back-and-forth.

```
G O I T H R P E R S F A V S M S
Y X Q U S I T U W H O L S P B P
T P F A T H G O D E R S O H L R
R R A I S E T O T R I N O S E A
I W S P I R I O S H M A F O P H
U X P O N E R A I S T Y T L E L
N T E Y O H G O W E R I N Y R Y
E H A F A T H E R P I I R T S T
S R T A F Y T I N I N R H Y O R
R E H E R S N I E E I L O L N N
P E H O L O N T H R T Y T O S I
W Y T I R I P S P I Y T Y H L Y
```

WORD BANK

GOD
FATHER
HOLY
ONE
PERSONS
SON
SPIRIT
THREE
TRINITY
TRIUNE

7

...IN GOD THE FATHER

GOD IS THE FATHER OF ALL

The First Article of the Apostles' Creed tells us that God is the Father of all. All people in all places are His children. You, too, are a special child of God. In the Word Bank are some of the places where God's children live. Find and circle the words in the word search. Be sure to look up-and-down and back-and-forth.

```
F R A N C E A A C A N I H C O
M C A A I S A A O M Q X M A E
N I R F S A I L P U C T E S W
I A F R I C A A S R A S X E N
A G R E E N R S A I N R I L E
C I E N A L U K P X A Q C I D
I A U I U G O A A Y D P O Z E
R C R A I B A R A I A O U A W
E A O E W A R B I A M N V R S
M N P A I L A R T S U A X B S
A A E S S O R L N E R G Z A N
O P X Q N R U S S I A U M I R
G R E E N L A N D I A H O D W
M S I C I R E L E A R S I N X
E X A E N I U G W E N N A I Y
```

WORD BANK

AFRICA
ALASKA
AMERICA
ARABIA
ASIA
AUSTRALIA
BRAZIL
CANADA
CHINA
EUROPE
FRANCE
GREENLAND
INDIA
ISRAEL
MEXICO
NEW GUINEA
RUSSIA
SWEDEN

A LOVING FATHER

In Luke 15:11–32, Jesus told a story about a loving father who welcomed back with love a son who had left home. Jesus told the story to show God's love for sinners who repent and come back to Him for forgiveness. God is your loving Father.

First place the words from the Word Bank into the story. Then use the numbers to find where each word fits into the crossword puzzle.

A (1) _____ had two sons. One day one (2) _____ went to his father. The son wanted the (3) _____ that he would inherit someday. The father (4) _____ the son what he wanted. The son went (5) _____.

The son (6) _____ all his money. When it was all gone, the boy had to take care of (7) _____. He remembered the (8) _____ he had left. The boy went back to ask his father if he could come back as a (9) _____.

The father met the boy with open (10) _____. He had a (11) _____ for his returned son.

"My son who was lost, has been (12) _____," said the father. In the same way, God welcomes sinners like you and me when we ask Him for (13) _____ from our sins.

WORD BANK
ARMS   MONEY
AWAY   PARTY
FATHER   PIGS
FORGIVENESS   SERVANT
FOUND   SON
GAVE   SPENT
HOME

CREATION

God is not just "mighty," He is "almighty." By His word, everything in heaven and earth was made. God also made you! Read the story of creation in Genesis 1:1–2:3 to find how it happened. Read the clues. Use the words from the Word Bank to finish the crossword puzzle.

Word Bank:
ANIMALS
BIRDS
CLOUDS
EARTH
FISH
FLOWERS
GRASS
MAN
MOON
OCEAN
TREES
STARS
SUN
WOMAN

1. They were named by Adam.
2. He is a grown-up boy.
3. This is the name of our planet.
4. It shines during the day.
5. It grows green on your lawn.
6. They swim in the water.
7. These bloom in the spring.
8. These float in the sky.
9. Many of these make a forest.
10. They twinkle at night.
11. Large bodies of water found around the earth.
12. It is a light for the night.
13. She is a grown-up girl.
14. They fly in the sky.

GOD TAKES CARE OF HIS CHILDREN

God takes care of His children. God takes care of you. The explanation of the First Article tells us that God gives us everything we need each day. The names of some of the things God gives us are listed in the Word Bank. See how many you can find in the word search. Be sure to look up-and-down and back-and-forth.

```
X M P O Z Q F Y V E S U S I M E
H E F O O E O G I S E O H S S T
B O D Y Q Y O E H N E R D R D O
G S N M A D D I S C H I L D N R
N I E V O L H F O E R A C R A D
I O A E K E L O O H C S S I H N
H U T A X P E T S C T I O N I E
T W O R U O L T S E I R F K R Y
O X G S O U L V F R I E N D S L
L M S N S U V Q S U M C D F D I
C C E O E Y N S E N S E S C V M
L E Y E S C H U R X I M O H A A
C H U H C R U H C Y Q V S U H F
P E P R O T E C T I O N T C Z A
H O M E O O M E E E F E E T V Q
```

WORD BANK

BODY
CHURCH
CLOTHING
DRINK
EARS
EYES
FAMILY
FEET
FOOD
FRIENDS
HANDS
HOME
LOVE
PETS
PROTECTION
SCHOOL
SENSES
SHOES
SOUL

God's Children Take Care of His World

The LORD God took [Adam] and put him in the Garden of Eden to work it and take care of it (Genesis 2:15). We, too, want to take good care of the world God made for us. One way we can do this is by recycling materials that can be used again. Can you think of other ways you can take good care of God's world? Fit the names of some of the things we can recycle into the crossword puzzle. (Each word has its own space.)

WORD BANK

ALUMINUM CANS
CARDBOARD
GLASS BOTTLES
MAGAZINES
NEWSPAPERS
PLASTIC CONTAINERS
SCRAP PAPER

THE NAMES OF JESUS

An angel brought good news to Joseph. Mary was going to have a baby. The baby's name would be "Jesus," which means "the Lord saves." Jesus was to be the "Christ"—the special, chosen one for whom God's people had been waiting. We learn about Jesus in the Second Article of the Apostles' Creed. Can you think of other names for Jesus from the Bible?

Find and circle the names for Jesus written in the Word Bank. Be sure to look up-and-down and back-and-forth.

```
E G O O D S H E P H E R D
G N A N G E L O F G O D O
E H R G J E S U S P Q R W
L C I N O W P J O D D S O
A H S I O A R E H P E H R
N R T K P Y A O R D A E D
T I M M A N U E L R V P U
R S M E H P E H A D I P S
U T A R E D E E M E R R E
T R N D E E M E B U U E D
H M E S S I A H X Q T D R
V I S O R O I V A S H S O
```

WORD BANK

ANGEL OF GOD
CHRIST
GOOD SHEPHERD
IMMANUEL
JESUS
KING
LAMB
MESSIAH
REDEEMER
SAVIOR
TRUTH
WAY
WORD

An Angel Comes to Mary

What happened when an angel from God came to Mary?
Read Luke 1:26–38. Thank God that Jesus came to be your Savior.

First fit the words from the Word Bank into the story. Then place the words from each line of the story into the crossword puzzle.

An angel named (1) _____ was sent by God to a town in Galilee called (2) _____ to a young woman named (3) _____.

The angel said, "(4) _____," … "the Lord is with you."

Mary was (5) _____ at the angel's words.

The angel said, "Do not be (6) _____, Mary, you have found (7) _____ with God. You will give birth to a Son and are to give Him the name (8) _____."

"How will this be?" Mary (9) _____.

The angel answered, "The Holy (10) _____ will come upon you, and the Holy One to be born will be called the Son of (11) _____."

"I am the Lord's (12) _____," Mary answered. "May it be to me as you have said."

WORD BANK

AFRAID
ASKED
FAVOR
GABRIEL
GOD
GREETINGS
JESUS
MARY
NAZARETH
SERVANT
SPIRIT
TROUBLED

JESUS' BIRTH

Read the story of Jesus' birth in Luke 2:1–20. Remember Jesus was born for you.

First fit the words from the Word Bank into the blank spaces, then place them into the crossword puzzle.

Mary and (1) _____ went to Bethlehem. When they got there, there was no room in the (2) _____.

(3) _____ was born in a stable. Mary wrapped him in (5) _____. His first bed was a (4) _____.

(6) _____ were watching their sheep. Suddenly an (7) _____ appeared to them and said "Do not be (8) _____ , I bring you good news of great (9) _____ that will be to all people. Today in the town of David a (10) _____ has been born to you."

Then the (11) _____ was filled with angels praising God and saying, "(12) _____ to God in the highest."

The shepherds hurried to (13) _____ to see Jesus. They spread the news of Jesus'(14) _____. They told all they met what they had (15) _____ and seen.

WORD BANK

AFRAID
ANGEL
BETHLEHEM
BIRTH
CLOTHS
GLORY
HEARD
INN
JESUS
JOSEPH
JOY
MANGER
SAVIOR
SHEPHERDS
SKY

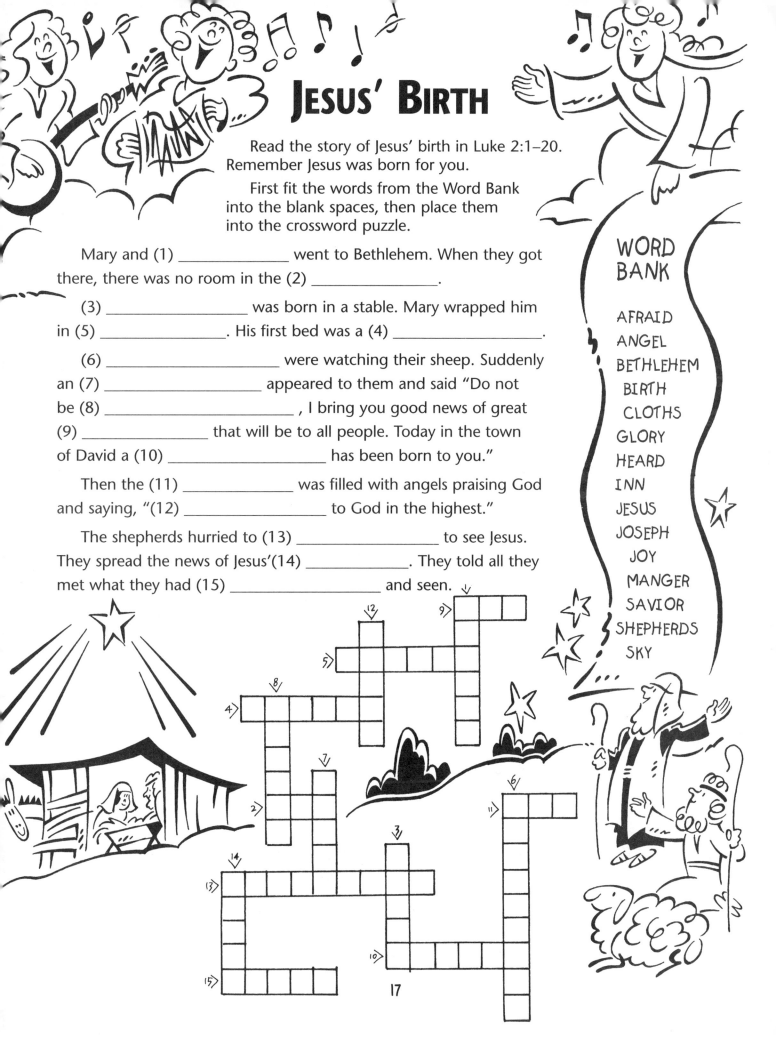

17

JOHN 3:16

Why did Jesus come to the earth? Here is what Jesus told Nicodemus:

"For **GOD** so **LOVED** the **WORLD** that He **GAVE** His **ONE** and **ONLY** **SON**, that **WHOEVER BELIEVES** in **HIM** shall not **PERISH** but have **ETERNAL LIFE**" (John 3:16).

Jesus came so that you might have eternal life.

Find the words written in **BOLD and CAPITAL LETTERS** from the verse above in the puzzle below. Be sure to look up-and-down and back-and-forth.

```
O L J O M C X E O N E Q X
G A V G O D E T E R N R J
L N G S E V E I L E B E V
R R D S O L O V E V T V W
O E D L R O W N T A H E P
W T S N O E S E H G W O E
E E B O L H A H T D O H F
H W E S I Y L N O L R W I
I O P E R I S H A G F I L
M V E S I L O V E D L I F
```

18

JESUS' BAPTISM

At the time of Jesus' Baptism, the Holy Spirit came down from heaven in the form of a dove and God the Father spoke. Follow the code to find out what God said.

A C D E F H I L M N O P R S T V W Y
1 2 3 4 5 6 7 8 9 10 11 12 13 14 15 16 17 18

___ ___ ___ ___ ___ ___ ___ ___ ___ ___ ___ ___ ___ ___ ___ ___ ___ ___ ___
1 10 3 1 16 11 7 2 4 5 13 11 9 6 4 1 16 4 10

___ ___ ___ ___ ___ ___ ___ ___ ___ ___ ___ ___ ___ ___ ___
14 1 7 3 15 6 7 14 7 14 9 18 14 11 10

___ ___ ___ ___ ___ ___ ___ ___ ___ ___ ___ ___ ___ ___ ___ ___
17 6 11 9 7 8 11 16 4 17 7 15 6 6 7 9

___ ___ ___ ___ ___ ___ ___ ___ ___ ___ ___ ___ ___ ___ ___
7 1 9 17 4 8 8 12 8 4 1 14 4 3

___ ___ ___ ___ ___ ___ ___ 3:17
9 1 15 15 6 4 17

Jesus' Trial

The time had come for Jesus to die on the cross. Read the story of Jesus before Pilate in Matthew 27:1–2,15–26. Jesus went to the cross in your place.

First fit the words from the Word Bank into the story, then use the numbers of each line to fit the words into the crossword puzzle.

WORD BANK

BARABBAS
CHRIST
CROWD
CRUCIFIED
FEAST
GOVERNOR
HANDS
JESUS
PILATE
PRISONER

Early in the morning, all the chief priests and elders of the people came to the decision to put (1) _____ to death. They bound Him, led Him away, and handed Him over to Pilate, the Roman (2) _____ .

Now it was the governor's custom at the (3) _____ to release a prisoner chosen by the crowd. At that time they had a notorious (4) _____, called Barabbas. So when the (5) _____ had gathered, (6) _____ asked them, "Which one do you want me to release to you: Barabbas, or Jesus who is called (7) _____?" The crowd chose (8) _____.

Then Pilate took water and washed his (9) _____ in front of the crowd. He released Barabbas to them. But he had Jesus flogged, and handed Him over to be (10) _____ .

JESUS' SUFFERING

PILATE'S SOLDIERS put a purple robe on [*JESUS*], then twisted together a **CROWN** of thorns and set it on Him. And they began to call out to Him, "Hail, **KING** of the **JEWS!**" Again and again they struck Him on the **HEAD** with a staff and spit on Him. Falling on their knees, they paid homage to **HIM**. And when they had **MOCKED** Him, they took off the **PURPLE** robe and put His own clothes on Him. Then they led Him out to crucify Him (Mark 15:17–20).

Why did Jesus let Pilate's soldiers do this to Him?

Fit each bolded and capitalized set of words from above into the blanks below. Read down the circled letters to find the words that complete the sentence to see how much Jesus loves you.

_ _ _ _ _
_ _ _ _ _ _ _
_ _ _ _ _
_ _ _ _
_ _ _

Jesus suffered under Pilate
to _____ **us**

_ _ _ _ _
_ _ _ _ _ _ _
_ _ _
_ _ _ _

from our _____ **.**

JESUS' DEATH

Read the story of Jesus' death in John 19:17–37.
He died that you might live eternally in heaven.

First fit the words from the Word Bank into the blank spaces, then use the number from each line to fit the words into the crossword puzzle.

Jesus was (1) _____ on a cross. He was placed between two (2) _____. (3) _____ had a sign put above Jesus' cross that read: "Jesus of Nazareth, (4) _____ of the Jews."

The soldiers cast lots for Jesus' (5) _____.

When all the (6) _____ had been fulfilled, Jesus said, "I am (7) _____." Someone held up a sponge soaked in (8) _____ for Jesus to drink. When He received the drink, Jesus said, "It is (9) _____." Then (10) _____ bowed His head and (11) _____ .

WORD BANK

CLOTHES
CRUCIFIED
DIED
FINISHED
JESUS
KING
OTHERS
PILATE
SCRIPTURE
THIRSTY
VINEGAR

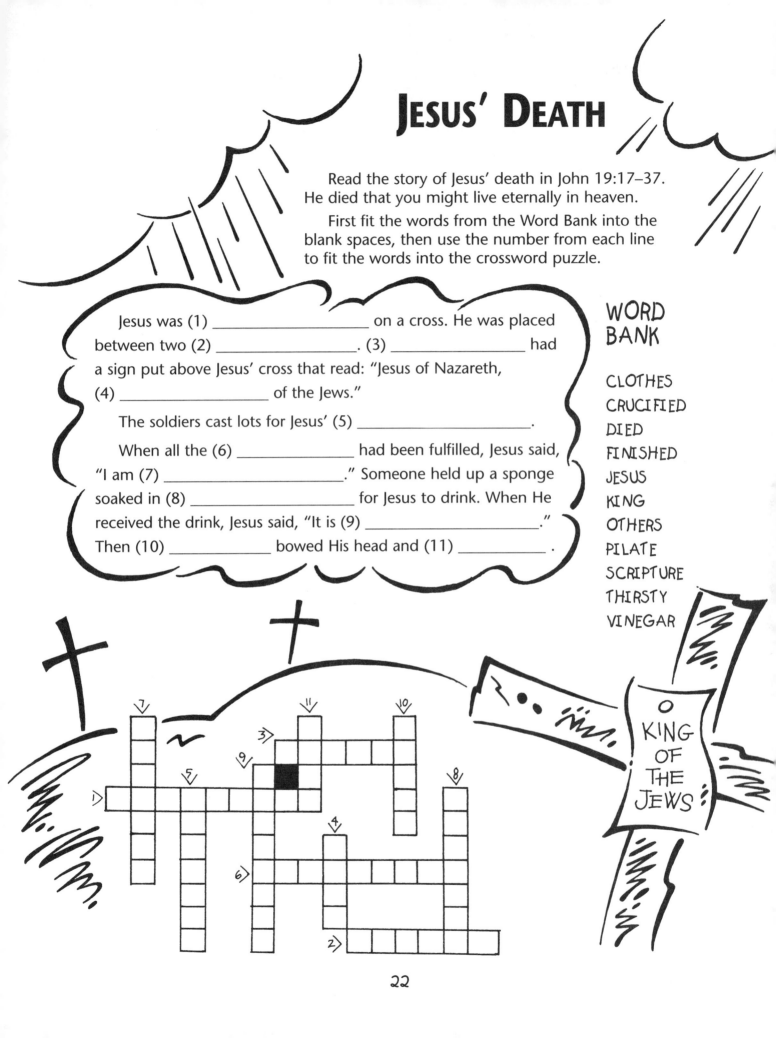

JESUS' BURIAL

Read the story of Jesus' burial in Matthew 27:57–60. First fit the words from the Word Bank into the blanks, then finish the puzzle.

As evening approached, there came a (1) _____ man from (2) _____, named (3) _____, who had himself become a disciple of Jesus. Going to (4) _____, he asked for Jesus' (5) _____. He took the body, wrapped it in a clean (6) _____ cloth, and placed it in his own new (7) _____ that he had cut out of a rock. He rolled a big (8) _____ in front of the entrance to the tomb and went away.

WORD BANK

ARIMATHEA
BODY
JOSEPH
LINEN
PILATE
RICH
STONE
TOMB

Do you know what happened next?

JESUS LIVES!

Jesus rose again, just as He said He would. Read what happened next in Luke 24:1–12. Finish the story of the first Easter by completing the following statements. Then use those words to complete the puzzle. Remember, Jesus lives for you!

1. It was the _____ day of the week, very early in the morning.

2. Some _____ went to Jesus' tomb.

3. They wanted to put the _____ they had prepared on Jesus' body for burial.

4. When they got to the tomb, they found the _____ rolled away.

5. Jesus' _____ was not inside.

6. Suddenly _____ men stood beside them.

7. The men's clothes gleamed like _____.

8. In their _____ the women fell down.

9. "Why do you look for the _____ among the dead?" asked the men.

10. "He is not here. He has _____!"

WORD BANK

BODY
FIRST
FRIGHT
LIGHTNING
LIVING
RISEN
SPICES
STONE
TWO
WOMEN

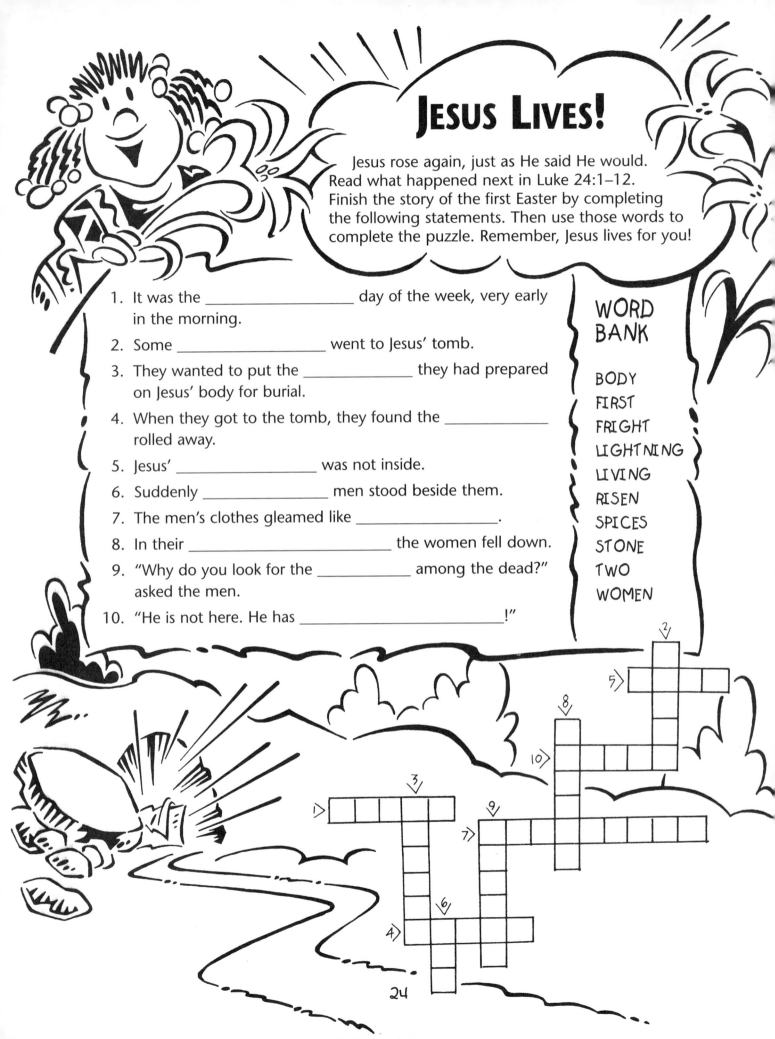

24

JESUS IS YOUR LORD TOO

Read John 20:24–29 to find out about a time when Jesus appeared to His disciples. This story tells us why we know that Jesus is our Lord too. Use words from the Word Bank to fill in the blanks and then fit them into the puzzle.

Thomas was not with the (1) _____ when Jesus (2) _____ to them. Thomas said he would not believe (3) _____ was alive unless he saw His hands and side.

A week later the disciples were together in the (4) _____ again, and (5) _____ was with them. Though the doors were (6) _____, Jesus came and (7) _____ among them and said, "(8) _____ be with you!" Then Jesus (9) _____ Thomas His hands and side and said, "Stop (10) _____ and believe."

Thomas said, "My (11) _____ and my (12) _____." Then Jesus said, "Because you have seen Me, you have (13) _____; (14) _____ are those who have not seen and yet have believed."

WORD BANK

BELIEVED
BLESSED
CAME
DISCIPLES
DOUBTING
GOD
HOUSE
JESUS
LOCKED
LORD
PEACE
SHOWED
STOOD
THOMAS

JESUS ASCENDED INTO HEAVEN

How did Jesus ascend into heaven? Read the story in Acts 1:3–12. Use the words from the Word Bank to fill in the blanks and then to finish the crossword puzzle. Remember, although you cannot see Him, Jesus is always with you.

It was (1) _____ days after Jesus' resurrection. Jesus and His (2) _____ were on the (3) _____ of (4) _____, outside of (5) _____. As Jesus was talking to the disciples, He was taken up before their very (6) _____ and a (7) _____ hid Him from their (8) _____.

As the disciples looked up into the (9) _____, suddenly (10) _____ men dressed in (11) _____ stood beside them saying, "(12) _____ of (13) _____, why do you stand here (14) _____ up into the sky? This same (15) _____ who has been taken from you into (16) _____, will come (17) _____ in the same (18) _____ you have seen Him go."

WORD BANK

BACK   CLOUD
DISCIPLES
EYES   FORTY
GALILEE

HEAVEN
JERUSALEM
JESUS
LOOKING
MEN   MOUNT
OLIVES   SIGHT
SKY   TWO
WAY   WHITE

A PLACE IN HEAVEN

Why did Jesus return to heaven? Read John 14:2 to find the answer. Use the code to read what Jesus said. Count the number of spaces forward and backward from the letter K.

WORD CODE

B = Backward   F = Forward

A B C D E F G H I J **K** L M N O P Q R S T U V W X Y Z

——— —— —— —————— —————————————— ,
B2 F3   F2 F14   B5 B10 F9 B3 B6 F7 F8   B3 F4 F10 F8 B6

—————— ———————————— —————————— ; . . .
B10 F7 B6   F2 B10 F3 F14   F7 F4 F4 F2 F8

—————— —————————— ————————
B2 B10 F2   B4 F4 B2 F3 B4   F9 B3 B6 F7 B6

———————————— ——————————————
F9 F4   F5 F7 B6 F5 B10 F7 B6   B10   F5 F1 B10 B8 B6

—————————— .
B5 F4 F7 F14 F4 F10

WHERE IS JESUS?

Where is Jesus now? In heaven, at God's right hand. In the Book of Revelation, John describes this wonderful sight. John heard all of creation sing these words to God:

*"To **HIM** who **SITS** on the **THRONE** and to the **LAMB** be **PRAISE** and **HONOR** and **GLORY** and **POWER**, for **EVER** and ever!"*

(Revelation 5:13b)

What words can you think of to use in praise of Jesus? Fit the bolded words from the verse above into the crossword blanks.

Jesus Will Come Again

Jesus told how He would come again to judge the world. Read Matthew 25:31–40 to find out how Jesus will come again to judge the world. Jesus will come again for you.

Fit the words from the Word Bank into the blanks, then use them to finish the crossword puzzle.

When the (1) _____ of Man comes in all His glory, and all the (2) _____ with Him, He will sit on His (3) _____ in heavenly (4) _____. All the (5) _____ will be gathered before Him, and He will separate the people one from another as a (6) _____ separates the sheep from the goats. He will put the (7) _____ on His right hand and the (8) _____ on His left.

Then the King will say to those on His right, "Come, you who are (9) _____ by My Father; … when I was (10) _____ you gave Me something to eat, I was (11) _____ and you gave Me something to drink, … whatever you did for one of the least of these (12) _____ of Mine, you did it for Me."

WORD BANK

ANGELS
BLESSED
BROTHERS
GLORY
GOATS
HUNGRY
NATIONS
SHEEP
SHEPHERD
SON
THIRSTY
THRONE

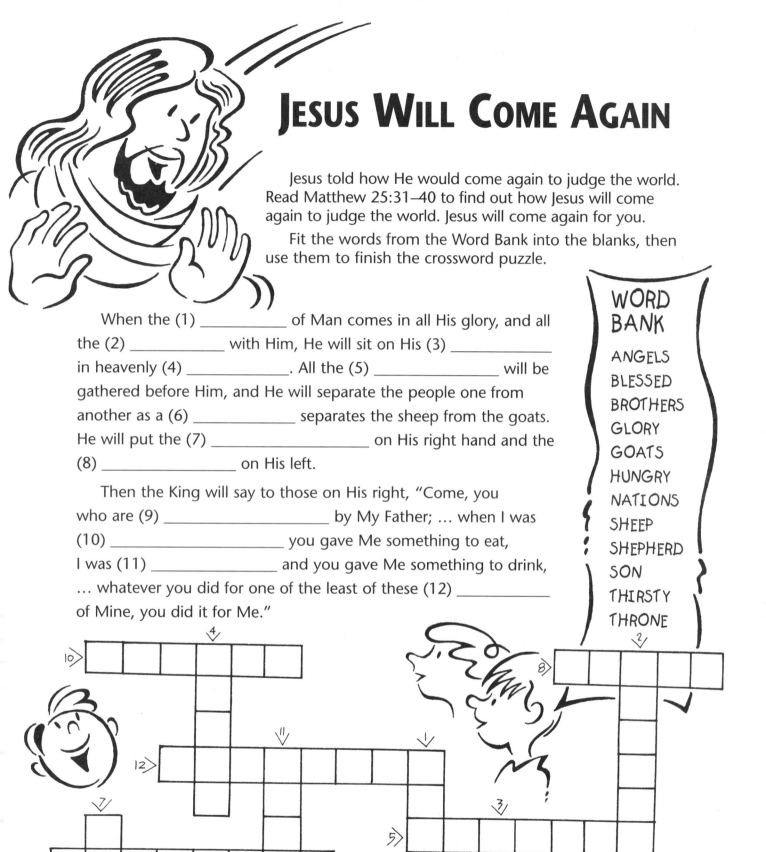

29

THE HOLY SPIRIT

Before He died, Jesus told His disciples that the Holy Spirit would come and comfort them after He was gone:

"But the COUNSELOR, the HOLY SPIRIT, whom the FATHER will SEND in My NAME, will TEACH you all THINGS and will REMIND you of EVERYTHING I have SAID to YOU"

(John 14:26).

The Holy Spirit gives you faith in Jesus as your Savior. We learn about the Holy Spirit in the Third Article of the Apostles' Creed.

Look for the words written in **BOLD and CAPITAL TYPE**. Be sure to look up-and-down and back-and-forth.

```
T D H E S A N C T I F I E E
M N S R C O U N S E L O R V
A I E D D D E H T A F E N E
K M N I S B Y H C A E T F R
E E D A P A N N A H T I A Y
S R C S I R A D B Y B A D T
U S H I R F M F A T H E R H
E Y O U I T E A W M S I Q I
H T D N T H I N G S X K N N
W O H O L Y R D W E T H A G
```

...IN THE HOLY CHRISTIAN CHURCH

PENTECOST

The Holy Spirit came in the form of a dove the day Jesus was baptized. Read Acts 2:1–12 to find out how the Holy Spirit came on the first Pentecost. The Holy Spirit also comes to God's children today through the Bible, Baptism, and the Lord's Supper. Use words from the Word Bank to finish the story and complete the crossword puzzle.

When the day of (1) _____ came, they were all together in one place. Suddenly a sound like the blowing of a violent (2) _____ came from heaven and filled the whole (3) _____ where they were sitting. They saw what seemed to be tongues of (4) _____ that separated and came to rest on each of them. All of them were (5) _____ with the (6) _____ Spirit and began to speak in other (7) _____ (languages) as the (8) _____ enabled them.

Now there were staying in Jerusalem God-fearing Jews from every (9) _____ under heaven. When they heard this sound, a crowd came together in bewilderment, because each one heard them speaking in his own (10) _____.

WORD BANK

FILLED
FIRE
HOLY
HOUSE
LANGUAGE
NATION
PENTECOST
SPIRIT
TONGUES
WIND

...IN THE
COMMUNION
OF SAINTS

INTRODUCING PAUL

In the Bible we read letters written by Paul to "the church of God in Corinth," as well as to "all those everywhere who call on the name of our Lord Jesus Christ." Paul's words remind us that we are part of the "Holy Christian church" on earth and all believers in Jesus who have ever lived—the "communion of saints." Because you believe in Jesus, you, too, are part of God's family, the church.

Here are the names of other cities where Paul might have written to Christians if he were alive today. Fit them into the crossword puzzle.

WORD BANK

BOSTON
CANBERRA
DENVER
DRESDEN
EDMONTON
KANSAS CITY
MADRAS
MONTEREY
MOSCOW
NAIROBI
OSLO
PARIS
PORTLAND
PRAGUE
SEWARD
WARSAW

...IN THE FORGIVENESS OF SINS

TWO MEN PRAYING

God forgives all sinners. Read in Luke 18:9–14 the story Jesus once told of two men praying in the temple. First fill in the blanks with words from the Word Bank, then use them to finish the puzzle.

WORD BANK

BEAT
COLLECTOR
DISTANCE
GOD
HEAVEN
HIMSELF
JESUS
JUSTIFIED
MEN
MERCY
PARABLE
PHARISEE
PRAYED
TEMPLE

(1) _____ told this (2) _____ (story): Two men went up to the (3) _____ to pray, one was a (4) _____ and the other a tax (5) _____. The Pharisee stood up and (6) _____ about (7) _____: "God, I thank You that I am not like other (8) _____—robbers, evildoers, adulterers—or even like this tax collector. I fast twice a week and give a tenth of all I get."

But the tax collector stood at a (9) _____. He would not even look up to (10) _____ , but (11) _____ his breast and said, "(12) _____, have (13) _____ on me, a sinner."

It was this tax collector that Jesus said went home (14) _____ before God.

37

...IN THE
RESURRECTION
OF THE BODY

JOB

The book of Job tells of Job's trust in God, even when bad things happened to him. Job 19:25–27 tells of Job's faith—that he would rise from the dead to see God with his own eyes. On the last day you will see Jesus with *your* own eyes.

Write the letter that comes **before** the letter written below each blank space to find out what Job said.

___ ___ ___ ___ ___ ___ ___ ___ ___ ___ ___
 J   L   O   P   X   U   I   B   U   N   Z

___ ___ ___ ___ ___ ___ ___ ___ ___ ___ ___ ___ ___'
 S   F   E   F   F   N   F   S   M   J   W   F   T

___ ___ ___ ___ ___ ___ ___ ___ ___ ___ ___ ___ ___ ___
 B   O   E   U   I   B   U   J   O   U   I   F   F   O   E

___ ___ ___ ___ ___ ___ ___ ___ ___ ___
 I   F   X   J   M   M   T   U   B   O   E

___ ___ ___ ___ ___ ___ ___ ___ ___ ___ ___ .
 V   Q   P   O   U   I   F   F   B   S   U   I

. . . ___ ___ ___ ___ ___ ___ ___ ___ ___ ___
     Z   F   U   J   O   N   Z   G   M   F   T   I

___ ___ ___ ___ ___ ___ ___ ___ ___ ___ ;
 J   X   J   M   M   T   F   F   H   P   E

___ ___ ___ ___ ___ ___ ___ ___ ___
 J   N   Z   T   F   M   G   X   J   M   M

___ ___ ___ ___ ___ ___ ___ ___ ___ ___
 T   F   F   I   J   N   X   J   U   I   N   Z

___ ___ ___ ___ ___ ___ ___ — ___ ' ___ ___ ___ ___ ___ ___
 P   X   O   F   Z   F   T   J   B   O   E   O   P   U

___ ___ ___ ___ ___ ___ ___ .
 B   O   P   U   I   F   S

...AND LIFE EVERLASTING

Jesus, Our Good Shepherd

Jesus loves us as a shepherd loves his sheep. Once Jesus said, *"My sheep listen to My voice; I know them, and they follow Me. I give them eternal life, and they shall never perish; no one can snatch them out of My hand"* (John 10:27–28). Someday Jesus, your Good Shepherd, will take you to live forever with Him in heaven.

Fit the words from the Word Bank into the puzzle.

WORD BANK

ETERNAL
FOLLOW
GIVE
KNOW
LIFE
LISTEN
NEVER
PERISH
SHEEP
VOICE

Answer Key

The God I Know and Trust

The wordplays in this book will help you learn what the Bible teaches about the God you know and trust.

Find and circle these words from the Apostles' Creed. Be sure to look up-and-down and back-and-forth.

WORD BANK

ALMIGHTY
BODY
BURIED
CHRIST
CHURCH
CRUCIFIED
DEAD
DESCENDED
EARTH
EVERLASTING
FATHER
GOD
HEAVEN
HOLY
JESUS
JUDGE
LIFE
LORD
MAKER
MARY
PILATE
RIGHT
ROSE
SAINTS
SON
SPIRIT
SUFFERED

5

God Is Three Persons

God is three Persons—Father, Son, and Holy Spirit—in one God. We call this God the "Holy Trinity" or "Triune God." This means "Three-in-One." You may have noticed that baptisms are done in the name of the Father, the Son, and the Holy Spirit.

Find and circle these words in the word search below. Be sure to look up-and-down and back-and-forth.

WORD BANK

GOD
FATHER
HOLY
ONE
PERSONS
SON
SPIRIT
THREE
TRINITY
TRIUNE

7

A Wonderful God

What a wonderful God we have. The Bible uses many words to describe God. Some of these words are listed below. Place these words about God into the crossword puzzle below. God is all these and more!

WORD BANK

ALMIGHTY
ETERNAL
FAIR
FAITHFUL
FORGIVING
GOOD

UNCHANGEABLE
HOLY
JUST
KIND
LOVE
MERCIFUL
SPIRIT

6

God Is the Father of All

The First Article of the Apostles' Creed tells us that God is the Father of all. All people in all places are His children. You, too, are a special child of God. In the Word Bank are some of the places where God's children live. Find and circle the words in the word search. Be sure to look up-and-down and back-and-forth.

WORD BANK

AFRICA
ALASKA
AMERICA
ARABIA
ASIA
AUSTRALIA
BRAZIL
CANADA
CHINA
EUROPE
FRANCE
GREENLAND
INDIA
ISRAEL
MEXICO
NEW GUINEA
RUSSIA
SWEDEN

9

42

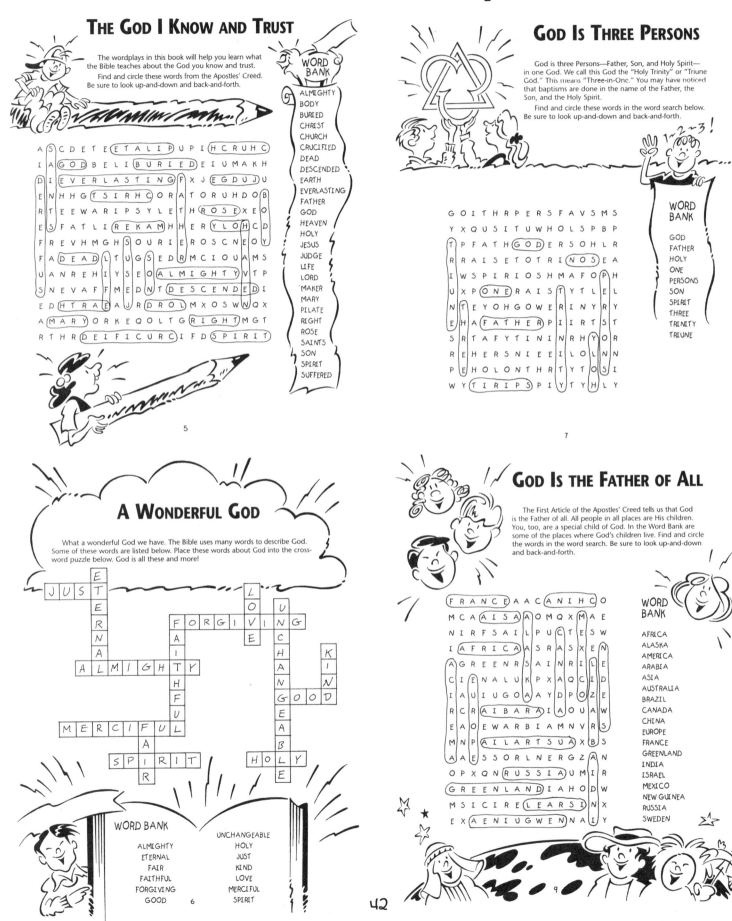

A Loving Father

In Luke 15:11–32, Jesus told a story about a loving father who welcomed back with love a son who had left home. Jesus told the story to show God's love for sinners who repent and come back to Him for forgiveness. God is your loving Father.

First place the words from the Word Bank into the story. Then use the numbers to find where each word fits into the crossword puzzle.

A (1) FATHER had two sons. One day one (2) SON went to his father. The son wanted the (3) MONEY that he would inherit someday. The father (4) GAVE the son what he wanted. The son went (5) AWAY.

The son (6) SPENT all his money. When it was all gone, the boy had to take care of (7) PIGS. He remembered the (8) HOME he had left. The boy went back to ask his father if he could come back as a (9) SERVANT.

The father met the boy with open (10) ARMS. He had a (11) PARTY for his returned son.

"My son who was lost, has been (12) FOUND," said the father. In the same way, God welcomes sinners like you and me when we ask Him for (13) FORGIVENESS from our sins.

WORD BANK
ARMS MONEY
AWAY PARTY
FATHER PIGS
FORGIVENESS SERVANT
FOUND SON
GAVE SPENT
HOME

God Takes Care of His Children

God takes care of His children. God takes care of you. The explanation of the First Article tells us that God gives us everything we need each day. The names of some of the things God gives us are listed in the Word Bank. See how many you can find in the word search. Be sure to look up-and-down and back-and-forth.

WORD BANK
BODY
CHURCH
CLOTHING
DRINK
EARS
EYES
FAMILY
FEET
FOOD
FRIENDS
HANDS
HOME
LOVE
PETS
PROTECTION
SCHOOL
SENSES
SHOES
SOUL

Creation

WORD BANK
ANIMALS
BIRDS
CLOUDS
EARTH
FISH
FLOWERS
GRASS
MAN
MOON
OCEAN
TREES
STARS
SUN
WOMAN

God is not just "mighty," He is "almighty." By His word, everything in heaven and earth was made. God also made you! Read the story of creation in Genesis 1:1–2:3 to find how it happened. Read the clues. Use the words from the Word Bank to finish the crossword puzzle.

1. They were named by Adam.
2. He is a grown-up boy.
3. This is the name of our planet.
4. It shines during the day.
5. It grows green on your lawn.
6. They swim in the water.
7. These bloom in the spring.
8. These float in the sky.
9. Many of these make a forest.
10. They twinkle at night.
11. Large bodies of water found around the earth.
12. It is a light for the night.
13. She is a grown-up girl.
14. They fly in the sky.

God's Children Take Care of His World

The LORD God took [Adam] and put him in the Garden of Eden to work it and take care of it (Genesis 2:15). We, too, want to take good care of the world God made for us. One way we can do this is by recycling materials that can be used again. Can you think of other ways you can take good care of God's world? Fit the names of some of the things we can recycle into the crossword puzzle. (Each word has its own space.)

WORD BANK
ALUMINUM CANS
CARDBOARD
GLASS BOTTLES
MAGAZINES
NEWSPAPERS
PLASTIC CONTAINERS
SCRAP PAPER

THE NAMES OF JESUS

An angel brought good news to Joseph. Mary was going to have a baby. The baby's name would be "Jesus," which means "the Lord saves." Jesus was to be the "Christ"—the special, chosen one for whom God's people had been waiting. We learn about Jesus in the Second Article of the Apostles' Creed. Can you think of other names for Jesus from the Bible?

Find and circle the names for Jesus written in the Word Bank. Be sure to look up-and-down and back-and-forth.

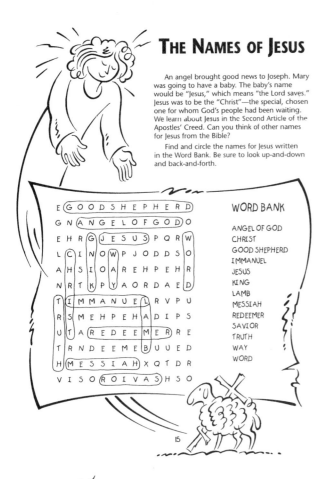

```
E G O O D S H E P H E R D
G N A N G E L O F G O D O
E H R G J E S U S P Q R W
L C I N O W P J O D D S O
A H S I O A R E H P E H R
N R T K P Y A O R D A E D
T I M M A N U E L R V P U
R S M E H P E H A D I P S
U T A R E D E E M E R R E
T R N D E E M E B U U E D
H M E S S I A H X Q T D R
V I S O R O I V A S H S O
```

WORD BANK

ANGEL OF GOD
CHRIST
GOOD SHEPHERD
IMMANUEL
JESUS
KING
LAMB
MESSIAH
REDEEMER
SAVIOR
TRUTH
WAY
WORD

15

JESUS' BIRTH

Read the story of Jesus' birth in Luke 2:1–20. Remember Jesus was born for you.

First fit the words from the Word Bank into the blank spaces, then place them into the crossword puzzle.

Mary and (1) _JOSEPH_ went to Bethlehem. When they got there, there was no room in the (2) _INN_.

(3) _JESUS_ was born in a stable. Mary wrapped him in (5) _CLOTHS_. His first bed was a (4) _MANGER_.

(6) _SHEPHERDS_ were watching their sheep. Suddenly an (7) _ANGEL_ appeared to them and said "Do not be (8) _AFRAID_, I bring you good news of great (9) _JOY_ that will be to all people. Today in the town of David a (10) _SAVIOR_ has been born to you."

Then the (11) _SKY_ was filled with angels praising God and saying, "(12) _GLORY_ to God in the highest."

The shepherds hurried to (13) _BETHLEHEM_ to see Jesus. They spread the news of Jesus'(14) _BIRTH_. They told all they met what they had (15) _HEARD_ and seen.

WORD BANK

AFRAID
ANGEL
BETHLEHEM
BIRTH
CLOTHS
GLORY
HEARD
INN
JESUS
JOSEPH
JOY
MANGER
SAVIOR
SHEPHERDS
SKY

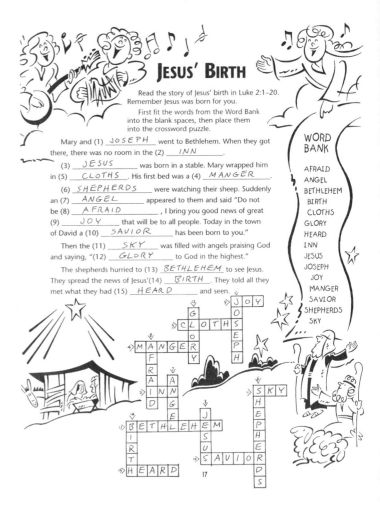

17

AN ANGEL COMES TO MARY

What happened when an angel from God came to Mary? Read Luke 1:26–38. Thank God that Jesus came to be your Savior.

First fit the words from the Word Bank into the story. Then place the words from each line of the story into the crossword puzzle.

An angel named (1) _GABRIEL_ was sent by God to a town in Galilee called (2) _NAZARETH_ to a young woman named (3) _MARY_.

The angel said, "(4) _GREETINGS_" ... "the Lord is with you." Mary was (5) _TROUBLED_ at the angel's words.

The angel said, "Do not be (6) _AFRAID_, Mary, you have found (7) _FAVOR_ with God. You will give birth to a Son and are to give Him the name (8) _JESUS_."

"How will this be?" Mary (9) _ASKED_.

The angel answered, "The Holy (10) _SPIRIT_ will come upon you, and the Holy One to be born will be called the Son of (11) _GOD_."

"I am the Lord's (12) _SERVANT_," Mary answered. "May it be to me as you have said."

WORD BANK

AFRAID
ASKED
FAVOR
GABRIEL
GOD
GREETINGS
JESUS
MARY
NAZARETH
SERVANT
SPIRIT
TROUBLED

16

JOHN 3:16

Why did Jesus come to the earth? Here is what Jesus told Nicodemus:

*"For **GOD** so **LOVED** the **WORLD** that He **GAVE** His **ONE** and **ONLY** **SON**, that **WHOEVER BELIEVES** in **HIM** shall not **PERISH** but have **ETERNAL LIFE**"* (John 3:16).

Jesus came so that you might have eternal life.

Find the words written in **BOLD** and **CAPITAL LETTERS** from the verse above in the puzzle below. Be sure to look up-and-down and back-and-forth.

```
O L J O M C X E O N E Q X
G A V G O D E T E R N R J
L N G S E V E I L E B E V
R R D S O L O V E V T V W
O E D L R O W N T A H E P
W T S N O E S E H G W O E
E E B O L H A H T D O H F
H W E S I Y L N O L R W I
I O P E R I S H A G F I L
M V E S I L O V E D L I F
```

18

44

JESUS' BAPTISM

At the time of Jesus' Baptism, the Holy Spirit came down from heaven in the form of a dove and God the Father spoke. Follow the code to find out what God said.

A	C	D	E	F	H	I	L	M	N	O	P	R	S	T	V	W	Y
1	2	3	4	5	6	7	8	9	10	11	12	13	14	15	16	17	18

A N D   A   V O I C E   F R O M   H E A V E N
1 10 3   1   16 11 7 2 4   5 13 11 9   6 4 1 16 4 10

S A I D   T H I S   I S   M Y   S O N
14 1 7 3   15 6 7 14   7 14   9 18   14 11 10

W H O M   I   L O V E   W I T H   H I M
17 6 11 9   7   8 11 16 4   17 7 15 6   6 7 9

I   A M   W E L L   P L E A S E D
7   1 9   17 4 8 8   12 8 4 1 14 4 3

M A T T H E W 3:17
9 1 15 15 6 4 17

JESUS' SUFFERING

PILATE'S SOLDIERS put a purple robe on [*JESUS*], then twisted together a **CROWN** of thorns and set it on Him. And they began to call out to Him, "Hail, **KING** of the **JEWS**!" Again and again they struck Him on the **HEAD** with a staff and spit on Him. Falling on their knees, they paid homage to **HIM**. And when they had **MOCKED** Him, they took off the **PURPLE** robe and put His own clothes on Him. Then they led Him out to crucify Him (Mark 15:17–20).

Why did Jesus let Pilate's soldiers do this to Him?

Fit each bolded and capitalized set of words from above into the blanks below. Read down the circled letters to find the words that complete the sentence to see how much Jesus loves you.

S O L D I E R S
M O C K E D
P U R P L E
H I M
C R O W N
H E A D

Jesus suffered under Pilate
to ___REDEEM___ us

J E S U S
P I L A T E'S
K I N G
J E W S

from our ___SINS___ .

21

JESUS' TRIAL

The time had come for Jesus to die on the cross. Read the story of Jesus before Pilate in Matthew 27:1–2,15–26. Jesus went to the cross in your place.

First fit the words from the Word Bank into the story, then use the numbers of each line to fit the words into the crossword puzzle.

WORD BANK

BARABBAS
CHRIST
CROWD
CRUCIFIED
FEAST
GOVERNOR
HANDS
JESUS
PILATE
PRISONER

Early in the morning, all the chief priests and elders of the people came to the decision to put (1) ___JESUS___ to death. They bound Him, led Him away, and handed Him over to Pilate, the Roman (2) ___GOVERNOR___.

Now it was the governor's custom at the (3) ___FEAST___ to release a prisoner chosen by the crowd. At that time they had a notorious (4) ___PRISONER___, called Barabbas. So when the (5) ___CROWD___ had gathered, (6) ___PILATE___ asked them, "Which one do you want me to release to you: Barabbas, or Jesus who is called (7) ___CHRIST___?" The crowd chose (8) ___BARABBAS___.

Then Pilate took water and washed his (9) ___HANDS___ in front of the crowd. He released Barabbas to them. But he had Jesus flogged, and handed Him over to be (10) ___CRUCIFIED___.

20

45

JESUS' DEATH

Read the story of Jesus' death in John 19:17–37. He died that you might live eternally in heaven.

First fit the words from the Word Bank into the blank spaces, then use the number from each line to fit the words into the crossword puzzle.

WORD BANK

CLOTHES
CRUCIFIED
DIED
FINISHED
JESUS
KING
OTHERS
PILATE
SCRIPTURE
THIRSTY
VINEGAR

Jesus was (1) ___CRUCIFIED___ on a cross. He was placed between two (2) ___OTHERS___. (3) ___PILATE___ had a sign put above Jesus' cross that read: "Jesus of Nazareth, (4) ___KING___ of the Jews."

The soldiers cast lots for Jesus' (5) ___CLOTHES___.

When all the (6) ___SCRIPTURE___ had been fulfilled, Jesus said, "I am (7) ___THIRSTY___." Someone held up a sponge soaked in (8) ___VINEGAR___ for Jesus to drink. When He received the drink, Jesus said, "It is (9) ___FINISHED___." Then (10) ___JESUS___ bowed His head and (11) ___DIED___.

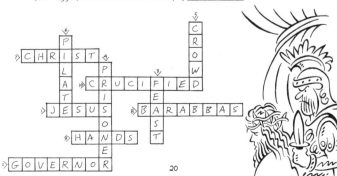

KING OF THE JEWS

22

Jesus' Burial

Read the story of Jesus' burial in Matthew 27:57–60. First fit the words from the Word Bank into the blanks, then finish the puzzle.

As evening approached, there came a (1) _RICH_ man from (2) _ARIMATHEA_, named (3) _JOSEPH_, who had himself become a disciple of Jesus. Going to (4) _PILATE_, he asked for Jesus' (5) _BODY_. He took the body, wrapped it in a clean (6) _LINEN_ cloth, and placed it in his own new (7) _TOMB_ that he had cut out of a rock. He rolled a big (8) _STONE_ in front of the entrance to the tomb and went away.

WORD BANK

ARIMATHEA
BODY
JOSEPH
LINEN
PILATE
RICH
STONE
TOMB

Do you know what happened next?

23

Jesus Is Your Lord Too

Read John 20:24–29 to find out about a time when Jesus appeared to His disciples. This story tells us why we know that Jesus is our Lord too. Use words from the Word Bank to fill in the blanks and then fit them into the puzzle.

Thomas was not with the (1) _DISCIPLES_ when Jesus (2) _CAME_ to them. Thomas said he would not believe (3) _JESUS_ was alive unless he saw His hands and side.

A week later the disciples were together in the (4) _HOUSE_ again, and (5) _THOMAS_ was with them. Though the doors were (6) _LOCKED_, Jesus came and (7) _STOOD_ among them and said, "(8) _PEACE_ be with you!" Then Jesus (9) _SHOWED_ Thomas His hands and side and said, "Stop (10) _DOUBTING_ and believe."

Thomas said, "My (11) _LORD_ and my (12) _GOD_." Then Jesus said, "Because you have seen Me, you have (13) _BELIEVED_; (14) _BLESSED_ are those who have not seen and yet have believed."

WORD BANK

BELIEVED
BLESSED
CAME
DISCIPLES
DOUBTING
GOD
HOUSE
JESUS
LOCKED
LORD
PEACE
SHOWED
STOOD
THOMAS

25

Jesus Lives!

Jesus rose again, just as He said He would. Read what happened next in Luke 24:1–12. Finish the story of the first Easter by completing the following statements. Then use those words to complete the puzzle. Remember, Jesus lives for you!

1. It was the _FIRST_ day of the week, very early in the morning.
2. Some _WOMEN_ went to Jesus' tomb.
3. They wanted to put the _SPICES_ they had prepared on Jesus' body for burial.
4. When they got to the tomb, they found the _STONE_ rolled away.
5. Jesus' _BODY_ was not inside.
6. Suddenly _TWO_ men stood beside them.
7. The men's clothes gleamed like _LIGHTNING_.
8. In their _FRIGHT_ the women fell down.
9. "Why do you look for the _LIVING_ among the dead?" asked the men.
10. "He is not here. He has _RISEN_!"

WORD BANK

BODY
FIRST
FRIGHT
LIGHTNING
LIVING
RISEN
SPICES
STONE
TWO
WOMEN

24

Jesus Ascended into Heaven

How did Jesus ascend into heaven? Read the story in Acts 1:3–12. Use the words from the Word Bank to fill in the blanks and then to finish the crossword puzzle. Remember, although you cannot see Him, Jesus is always with you.

It was (1) _FORTY_ days after Jesus' resurrection. Jesus and His (2) _DISCIPLES_ were on the (3) _MOUNT_ of (4) _OLIVES_, outside of (5) _JERUSALEM_. As Jesus was talking to the disciples, He was taken up before their very (6) _EYES_ and a (7) _CLOUD_ hid Him from their (8) _SIGHT_.

As the disciples looked up into the (9) _SKY_, suddenly (10) _TWO_ men dressed in (11) _WHITE_ stood beside them saying, "(12) _MEN_ of (13) _GALILEE_, why do you stand here (14) _LOOKING_ up into the sky? This same (15) _JESUS_ who has been taken from you into (16) _HEAVEN_, will come (17) _BACK_ in the same (18) _WAY_ you have seen Him go."

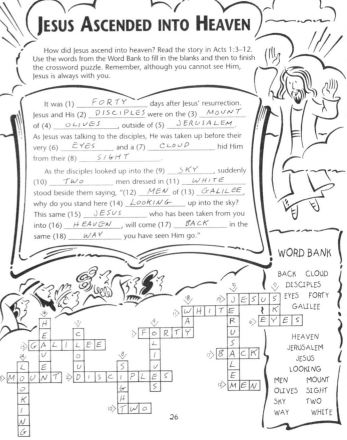

WORD BANK

BACK CLOUD
DISCIPLES
EYES FORTY
GALILEE

HEAVEN
JERUSALEM
JESUS
LOOKING
MEN MOUNT
OLIVES SIGHT
SKY TWO
WAY WHITE

26

46

A Place in Heaven

Why did Jesus return to heaven? Read John 14:2 to find the answer. Use the code to read what Jesus said. Count the number of spaces forward and backward from the letter K.

WORD CODE

B = Backward   F = Forward

A B C D E F G H I J **K** L M N O P Q R S T U V W X Y Z

I N   M Y   F A T H E R ' S   H O U S E
B2 F3 F2 F14 B5 B10 F9 B3 B6 F7 F8 B3 F4 F10 F8 B6

A R E   M A N Y   R O O M S ; . . .
B10 F7 B6 F2 B10 F3 F14 F7 F4 F4 F2 F8

I   A M   G O I N G   T H E R E
B2 B10 F2 B4 F4 B2 F3 B4 F9 B3 B6 F7 B6

T O   P R E P A R E   A   P L A C E
F9 F4 F5 F7 B6 F5 B10 F7 B6 B10 F5 F1 B10 B8 B6

F O R   Y O U .
B5 F4 F7 F14 F4 F10

27

Where Is Jesus?

Where is Jesus now? In heaven, at God's right hand. In the Book of Revelation, John describes this wonderful sight. John heard all of creation sing these words to God:

"To HIM who SITS on the THRONE and to the LAMB be PRAISE and HONOR and GLORY and POWER, for EVER and ever!"

(Revelation 5:13b)

What words can you think of to use in praise of Jesus? Fit the bolded words from the verse above into the crossword blanks.

H
I
G L A M B
O
P O W E R
E V E R Y
R
A
I
S I T S
E
T H R
H O N O R
N
E

28

Jesus Will Come Again

Jesus told how He would come again to judge the world. Read Matthew 25:31–40 to find out how Jesus will come again to judge the world. Jesus will come again for you.

Fit the words from the Word Bank into the blanks, then use them to finish the crossword puzzle.

When the (1) _SON_ of Man comes in all His glory, and all the (2) _ANGELS_ with Him, He will sit on His (3) _THRONE_ in heavenly (4) _GLORY_. All the (5) _NATIONS_ will be gathered before Him, and He will separate the people one from another as a (6) _SHEPHERD_ separates the sheep from the goats. He will put the (7) _SHEEP_ on His right hand and the (8) _GOATS_ on His left.

Then the King will say to those on His right, "Come, you who are (9) _BLESSED_ by My Father; … when I was (10) _HUNGRY_ you gave Me something to eat, I was (11) _THIRSTY_ and you gave Me something to drink, … whatever you did for one of the least of these (12) _BROTHERS_ of Mine, you did it for Me."

WORD BANK

ANGELS
BLESSED
BROTHERS
GLORY
GOATS
HUNGRY
NATIONS
SHEEP
SHEPHERD
SON
THIRSTY
THRONE

10) H U N G R Y
G
L
O
12) B R O T H E R S
S
S H E P H E R D
E
E
P

8) G O A T S
N
G
E
L
3) ...
5) N A T I O N S
H
R
O
N
E
9) B L E S S E D

29

The Holy Spirit

Before He died, Jesus told His disciples that the Holy Spirit would come and comfort them after He was gone:

"But the COUNSELOR, the HOLY SPIRIT, whom the FATHER will SEND in My NAME, will TEACH you all THINGS and will REMIND you of EVERYTHING I have SAID to YOU"

(John 14:26).

The Holy Spirit gives you faith in Jesus as your Savior. We learn about the Holy Spirit in the Third Article of the Apostles' Creed.

Look for the words written in **BOLD and CAPITAL TYPE.** Be sure to look up-and-down and back-and-forth.

T D H E S A N C T I F I E E
M N S R C O U N S E L O R V
A I E D D E H T A F E N E
K M N I S B Y H C A E T F R
E E D A P A N N A H T I A Y
S R C S I R A D B Y B A D T
U S H I R F M F A T H E R H
E Y O U I T E A W M S I Q I
H T D N T H I N G S X K N N
W O H O L Y R D W E T H A G

31

Pentecost

The Holy Spirit came in the form of a dove the day Jesus was baptized. Read Acts 2:1–12 to find out how the Holy Spirit came on the first Pentecost. The Holy Spirit also comes to God's children today through the Bible, Baptism, and the Lord's Supper. Use words from the Word Bank to finish the story and complete the crossword puzzle.

When the day of (1) _PENTECOST_ came, they were all together in one place. Suddenly a sound like the blowing of a violent (2) _WIND_ came from heaven and filled the whole (3) _HOUSE_ where they were sitting. They saw what seemed to be tongues of (4) _FIRE_ that separated and came to rest on each of them. All of them were (5) _FILLED_ with the (6) _HOLY_ Spirit and began to speak in other (7) _TONGUES_ (languages) as the (8) _SPIRIT_ enabled them.

Now there were staying in Jerusalem God-fearing Jews from every (9) _NATION_ under heaven. When they heard this sound, a crowd came together in bewilderment, because each one heard them speaking in his own (10) _LANGUAGE_.

WORD BANK

FILLED
FIRE
HOLY
HOUSE
LANGUAGE
NATION
PENTECOST
SPIRIT
TONGUES
WIND

33

Two Men Praying

God forgives all sinners. Read in Luke 18:9–14 the story Jesus once told of two men praying in the temple. First fill in the blanks with words from the Word Bank, then use them to finish the puzzle.

(1) _JESUS_ told this (2) _PARABLE_ (story): Two men went up to the (3) _TEMPLE_ to pray, one was a (4) _PHARISEE_ and the other a tax (5) _COLLECTOR_. The Pharisee stood up and (6) _PRAYED_ about (7) _HIMSELF_: "God, I thank You that I am not like other (8) _MEN_ —robbers, evildoers, adulterers— or even like this tax collector. I fast twice a week and give a tenth of all I get."

But the tax collector stood at a (9) _DISTANCE_. He would not even look up to (10) _HEAVEN_, but (11) _BEAT_ his breast and said, "(12) _GOD_, have (13) _MERCY_ on me, a sinner."

It was this tax collector that Jesus said went home (14) _JUSTIFIED_ before God.

WORD BANK

BEAT
COLLECTOR
DISTANCE
GOD
HEAVEN
HIMSELF
JESUS
JUSTIFIED
MEN
MERCY
PARABLE
PHARISEE
PRAYED
TEMPLE

37

Introducing Paul

In the Bible we read letters written by Paul to "the church of God in Corinth," as well as to "all those everywhere who call on the name of our Lord Jesus Christ." Paul's words remind us that we are part of the "Holy Christian church" on earth and all believers in Jesus who have ever lived— the "communion of saints." Because you believe in Jesus, you, too, are part of God's family, the church.

Here are the names of other cities where Paul might have written to Christians if he were alive today. Fit them into the crossword puzzle.

WORD BANK

BOSTON
CANBERRA
DENVER
DRESDEN
EDMONTON
KANSAS CITY
MADRAS
MONTEREY
MOSCOW
NAIROBI
OSLO
PARIS
PORTLAND
PRAGUE
SEWARD
WARSAW

35

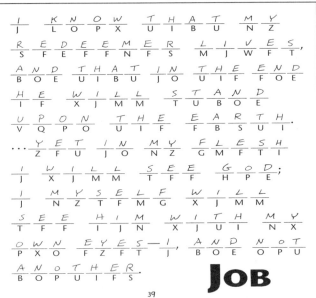

I KNOW THAT MY
J LOPX UIBU NZ

REDEEMER LIVES,
SFEFFNFS MJWFT,

AND THAT IN THE END
BOE UIBU JO UIF FOE

HE WILL STAND
IF XJMM TUBOE

UPON THE EARTH.
VQPO UIF FBSUI.

...YET IN MY FLESH
ZFU JO NZ GMFTI

I WILL SEE GOD;
J XJMM TFF HPE;

I MYSELF WILL
J NZTFMG XJMM

SEE HIM WITH MY
TFF IJN XJUI NZ

OWN EYES—I, AND NOT
PXO FZFT—J, BOE OPU

ANOTHER.
BOPUIFS.

JOB

39

Jesus, Our Good Shepherd

WORD BANK

ETERNAL
FOLLOW
GIVE
KNOW
LIFE
LISTEN
NEVER
PERISH
SHEEP
VOICE

41

48